Images of
Congaree National Park
Hopkins, South Carolina

Compiled by
Carolinas' Nature Photographers Association
and
Friends of Congaree Swamp

Bald Cypress — Rhonda Grego

Distributed by:
Carolinas' Nature Photographers Association
Post Office Box 245
Williston, SC 29853

Published by:  TOTALLY OUTDOORS PUBLISHING, INC.

Printed and bound by: Friesens, Altona, Manitoba, Canada

Library of Congress #2004099412
64 pages
114 color photographs

ISBN #0-9726653-2-3
UPC #85675500010

Book Committee:
LaBruce Alexander   Mary Kelly
Drew Eschbacher   Betty Mandell
Doug Gardner   Virginia Winn

Layout and Design: Virginia E. Winn

Photo Credits:
Cover: Cypress-Tupelo Floodplain by Andrew E. Eschbacher
Title page: Reflections by Virginia E. Winn
Page 3: Harry Hampton's photograph was provided by his daughter, Harriott Hampton Faucette

Thanks to the following for their assistance:
Martha Bogle, Superintendent of Congaree National Park, for her active support and encouragement. CW4 Allan J. Watkins for donating his time and piloting expertise which allowed us to obtain aerial images of the Congaree National Park and Congaree River. John Cely, John Nelson, John Grego, Robin Carter, Lynn B. Smith, Mary Garland Douglass, Tom Jones, and Janet Ciegler for assisting with plant and animal identification. John Cely and Mark Kinzer for verifying the historical background. Doug Gardner for allowing us to publish through his company. Sharon Kelly for assisting with editing.

Cedar Creek — Joseph C. Kegley

Introduction

Dry, sandy pine uplands. Soggy cypress-tupelo bottomlands. The Congaree River. These are the interconnected ecosystems that define Congaree National Park's 22,000-plus acres.

The park is home to the largest old-growth bottomland hardwood forest left on the East Coast. This stand of 12,000 acres is one of the few remaining of the more than 50 million acres of hardwood forests that once lined rivers in the Southeast. Preserved among those 12,000 acres are national champion water hickory and loblolly pine trees and a Shumard oak that soon will be added to the list. The park also boasts sweet gum, laurel oak, persimmon, overcup oak, American holly, bald cypress and swamp chestnut trees that are the largest in the state.

The trees are here to enjoy today because of the efforts of Harry Hampton and a group of young conservationists who stood against the timber companies and hunt clubs to save the mysterious, wild riverlands from the loggers' saws. Logging operations in the area had ceased in 1914, but began again in 1969 on what was then private land. Hampton and

Harry Hampton

his small band launched a fervent campaign to educate the public to the impending loss of the majestic old trees.

In 1975, more than 700 people attended a day-long rally in Columbia to call for "Congaree Action Now." Later that year, a report by the S.C. Wildlife and Marine Resources Department affirmed the significance of the old-growth forest less than 20 miles from South Carolina's capital city of Columbia.

Through the efforts of South Carolina Senators Ernest "Fritz" Hollings and Strom Thurmond, along with Representative Floyd Spence, Congress created the Congaree Swamp National Monument in 1976, which brought the area into the National Park System and ensured protection for its environmental treasures.

Sen. Hollings and Rep. James Clyburn were successful in winning a national park designation for the monument in 2003. It also has been recognized as a National Natural Landmark, an International Biosphere Preserve, a Wilderness Area and a Globally Important Bird Area.

There are about 80 species of trees and 50 species of shrubs within the park, making it one of the most floristically diverse of the nearly 400 units of the National Park System. The tree canopy compares with that of the Amazon Basin.

Within the park, Nature has her way. All of the park's creatures and plants live out their life cycles with a minimum of human impact. When heavy rains swell the Congaree River, floodwaters and silt nourish the rich abundance of organisms found in the bottomland. When drought prevails, life adjusts accordingly.

Scientists and students have been researching the Congaree floodplain for more than 50 years, measuring and recording the interaction of plants, animals, and climate in this unique place. Much of its history is visible today, from the stumps of huge bald cypress trees logged in the late 1800s and early 1900s to the path of fallen trees cut down by Hurricane Hugo in 1989, to the normal cycles of life and death.

A visit to Congaree National Park cannot fail to remind us of William Ashworth's words that we are "a part of life too, one small thread in the broad, green fabric of the biosphere; and if we have forgotten that with our minds, we remember it with our bodies and souls."

We can learn much from Congree, just by being there, just by watching and listening.

The inspiration for this book arose out of the desire to share this special place. A collaborative group from the Columbia region of the Carolinas' Nature Photographers Association and the Friends of Congaree Swamp worked for almost four years to compile this book.

The pictures on the following pages provide a window into the park's vegetation and its creatures, many of which can easily be missed by the casual visitor. They illustrate the intricate interdependency of all living things and serve as a humble reminder of our connection to the Earth. Enjoy.

May 2005

Lower Boardwalk

Leo Rose

Historical Timeline

1540 Spanish explorer Hernando de Soto travels past the northern edge of the Congaree Swamp

1566 and **1567** Spanish explorer Juan Pardo crosses the Congaree Swamp on two exploratory expeditions from the coast

1587 Spanish settlers abandon the colony of Santa Elena on Parris Island

1670 England establishes Charles Towne

1701 English explorer John Lawson travels up the east bank of the Wateree River

1740s Settlers near Congaree Swamp begin to build roads and ferry systems

1752 Joyner's Ferry in operation on the Congaree River, near present-day US Highway 601; Later operated by John McCord

1781 Combatants in Revolutionary War cross back and forth over Congaree River at McCord's Ferry

1781 Francis Marion (the Swamp Fox) and Light Horse Harry Lee capture the British post at Ft. Motte, on the south side of the Congaree River in May

1783 Revolutionary War ends

1786 Isaac Huger begins construction of a ferry system about six miles upstream from McCord's Ferry

1786 South Carolina General Assembly creates city of Columbia, designates it the new state capital

Ca. **1830s** James Adams constructs dike(s) in Congaree Swamp

Ca. **1840s** First cattle mound built within Congaree Swamp

1842 Railroad from Branchville to Columbia completed

1865 Union and Confederate troops skirmish at Bates Ferry (formerly McCord's Ferry)

1897 Logging of virgin cypress begins in Congaree Swamp

1899–1918 Francis Beidler acquires parcels of swamp land along the north bank of the Congaree River; Logging of virgin cypress continues

1914 Logging operations cease in Beidler Tract

1969 Renewed logging in Beidler Tract sparks the campaign to preserve the Congaree Swamp

1975 Congaree Swamp National Preserve Association organizes a public rally to support swamp protection

1976 Congress establishes the **Congaree Swamp National Monument**

1983 Congaree Swamp National Monument designated an **International Biosphere Reserve**

1988 Congress authorizes boundary expansion and designates majority of monument as **wilderness**

1989 Hurricane Hugo strikes the swamp

2001 Congaree Swamp designated a **Globally Important Bird Area**

2001 Completion and dedication of the Harry Hampton Visitors' Center

2003 Congress authorizes boundary expansion

2003 Congress changes designation of monument to **Congaree National Park**

(left margin vertical labels: 1500s 1600s 1700s 1800s 1900s 2000s)

Bird's-eye view of the Congaree River

Virginia E. Winn

Looking north from Congaree Bluff Heritage Preserve into Congaree National Park

William L. Graf

Known as "the redwoods of the east," bald cypress trees tower over the forest canopy.

Bald Cypress
Rhonda Grego

Carex   Lisel Shoffner

Red Mulberry   Lisel Shoffner

Five-lined Skink   Leo Rose

Upper Boardwalk

J. Steven Faucette

South Carolina's first National Park and the nation's 57th, Congaree National Park ranks among the most diverse forests in the world. Even the difference of a few inches in elevation can alter the types of plants and animals found here.

Red Maple in Early Spring
Betty Mandell

Carolina Bog Mint
Lisel Shoffner

Wood Duck

Doug Gardner

Tupelo
Nicholas J. Moore

Spring Foliage
Blake Prince

Beaver
Jerry Bright

Signs of beaver activity
Joseph C. Kegley

Beaver Den
Richard Sassnett

Lower Boardwalk   Linda Lee

Slough   Carolyn Brauer Hudson

Wise Lake   Carolyn Brauer Hudson

Lower Boardwalk

Andrew E. Eschbacher

William L. Graf

William L. Graf

Views of Congaree River

William L. Graf

The year 2003 saw a long and heavy rainy season with unusually high water levels.

Upper Boardwalk
Andrew E. Eschbacher

Congaree River at flood stage
Susan Dugan

Part of Congaree National Park is a bottomland hardwood floodplain which averages about 10 floods a year, usually in winter and early spring.

Spring Floods on Cedar Creek

Andrew E. Eschbacher

Great Blue Heron   Allen Sharpe

Yellow-crowned Night Heron   Allen Sharpe

Anhinga   Allen Sharpe

Bald Cypress
Lisel Shoffner

Yellow Jessamine · Allen Sharpe

Pinxter Flower Azalea · George Xenakis

Cardinal Flower · Lisel Shoffner

Red-shouldered Hawk · Casey Szocinski

Osprey · Allen Sharpe

Swallow-tailed Kite · Richard Sassnett

Designated as a Globally Important Bird Area in 2001, the Park gives refuge to both permanent and migratory songbirds and birds of prey.

Immature Red-tailed Hawk · J. and D. Wuori

Slaty Skimmer

Leo Rose

Wood Thrush
Carl E. Moser

Chinese Mantis   Carl E. Moser

Writing Spider   Leo Rose

Bald-faced Hornets' Nest   Leo Rose

Imperial Moth Caterpillar   Joan Taylor

Sunset over the Congaree

Blake Prince

Luna Moth

Allen Sharpe

Sulfur Tuft

Lisel Shoffner

Turkey-tail Scott Sutter

Fading Scarlet Waxy Cap Lisel Shoffner

Turkey-tail Betty Mandell

Lower Boardwalk
Nicholas J. Moore

Raccoon

Blake Prince

Cedar Creek
Mark Henry McLane

Cottonmouth — Mark Henry McLane

Redbelly Water Snake — Doug Gardner

Broadheaded Skink — Leo Rose

Eastern Box Turtle — Allen Sharpe

Tip-ups, also known as "Harricanes"

Andrew E. Eschbacher

Butterweed

J. Steven Faucette

Butterweed

Joseph C. Kegley

Prothonotary Warbler

Doug Gardner

Lizard's-tail
Patrick D. McMillian

Green Tree Frog

Roumen Vesselinov

Insert: Banded Net-wing Beetle
Lisel Shoffner

Cypress-Tupelo Floodplain
Lisel Shoffner

Doe   Doug Gardner

White-tailed Deer

Fawn   Allen Sharpe

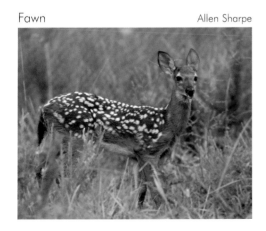

Buck   Doug Gardner

Cecropia Moth

Allen Sharpe

Walking Red Maple
Leo Rose

Assassin Bug   Leo Rose

Loblolly Pine   Andrew E. Eschbacher

Shagbark Hickory

Virginia E. Winn

Immature Screech Owls
Carl E. Moser

Great-horned Owl
Carl E. Moser

Barred Owl
Gary W. Carter

Screech Owl
Carl E. Moser

Insert: Fall Leaves   Betty Mandell

Upper Boardwalk

Betty Mandell

Slough
Caroline Brauer Hudson

Palamedes, Spicebush,
and Eastern Tiger Swallowtails

Allen Sharpe

Long-tailed Skipper

Allen Sharpe

Red Spotted Purple

George Xenakis

Gulf Fritillary

Virginia E. Winn

Pine Warbler   Gary W. Carter

White-eyed Vireo   Richard Sassnett

Eastern Pheobe   Richard Sassnett

Hermit Thrush   Gary W. Carter

Cypress-Tupelo Reflections

Lisel Shoffner

Long-leaf Pine   Rhonda Grego

There are at least 22 different
plant communities within
Congaree National Park.

Loblolly Pine
J. Steven Faucette

Abandoned Borrow Pit   Virginia E. Winn

Dwarf Palmetto   Leonard C. Vaughan

Cypress-Tupelo Floodplain   Leonard C. Vaughan

Red-headed Woodpecker   Carl E. Moser

Red-bellied Woodpecker
D. and J. Wuori

Insert: Bald Cypress
Allen Sharpe

Lower Boardwalk

Betty Mandell

Yaupon Holly Berries
Carol K. Tittle

Immature Piliated Woodpeckers

Doug Gardner

Downy Woodpecker  Casey Szocinski

Yellow-bellied Sapsucker Casey Szocinski

Marsh Rabbit
Leo Rose

Opossum   Doug Gardner

Feral Hog Piglet   Joseph C. Kegley

Wild Turkey   Doug Gardner

Cypress Knees
Andrew E. Eschbacher